PERDUTA GENTE

PETER READING

Secker & Warburg
POETRY

First published in Great Britain 1989
by Martin Secker & Warburg Limited
Michelin House, 81 Fulham Road, London SW3 6RB

Copyright © Peter Reading 1989

British Library Cataloguing in Publication Data

Reading, Peter, *1946–*
Perduta gente
I. Title
821'.914

ISBN 0 436 40999 2

Printed and bound in Great Britain by
Redwood Burn Limited, Trowbridge, Wiltshire

South Bank: Sibelius 5's
incontrovertible end –
five exhalations, bray of expiry,
        absolute silence…

Under the Festival Hall is a foetid
        tenebrous concert
strobed by blue ambulance light.
    PVC/newspapers/rags
insulate ranks of expendables, eyesores,
        winos, unworthies,
one of which (stiff in its cardboard Electrolux
        box stencilled **FRAGILE,**
    STOW THIS WAY UP, USE NO HOOKS)
officers lug to the tumbril,
    exhaling, like ostlers, its scents:

                squit,

                honk,

                piss,

                meths,

                distress.

London's most exciting apartments
all have river views, £330,000 to £865,000

"Large homes standing in two or three acres are now selling for well in excess of £200,000," Mr Williams said.

"That means there is no shortage of people willing to pay a relatively high price for old barns so they can do them up. At the end of the day, they will have a substantial home set in several acres worth a good deal more than £200,000."

Derelict barns in south Shropshire are fetching six figure prices — and estate agents say there are no shortage of interested buyers.

A ruin at Eastham, near Tenbury, with no roof and hardly any walls is on offer for £100,000.

And an L-shaped barn with an acre of land near Worfield saw some fierce bidding between two developers before finally going under the hammer for £222,000.

Money is no object to buyers seeking a quiet country life.

A large barn at Cleobury Mortimer occupying a commanding position at the end of a mile long track has just sold for £90,000.

Another site at nearby Milson, involving the conversion of three barns standing on an acre of land, sold at £167,000.

do s s

Talk Terms Today
OR REGRET IT FOR THE REST OF YOUR LIFE

JUSTHOME

Thank You

One day a lone hag gippo arrived and
        camped on the waste ground
which we traversed on our way to the school bus
        every morning.

Cumulus breath puffs rose from a pink-nosed
        rope-tethered skewbald.
Winter: a frost fern fronded the iced glass
        caravan window
through which I ventured a peep, but I leapt back
        horribly startled
    when the rime cleared and an eye
    glared through the hole at my own.
(Filthy she was, matted hair, withered leg and
        stank of excreta.)

After that, each time we passed it we'd lob a
        rock at the window.
When it was smashed she replaced it with cardboard;
        one of us lit it –
she hobbled round with a pisspot and doused the
        flames with its contents.
Then she gave up and just left it a gaping
        black fenestration
    through which we chucked bits of scrap,
    rubbish, a dog turd, a brick.

But when she skedaddled, a stain,
delineating where she'd been,
etiolated and crushed,
blighted that place, and remained.

Now we arrive at the front of the ruin;
*   here are there moanings,*
* shrieks, lamentations and dole,*
* here is there naught that illumes.*
Mucky Preece lives in a pigsty beside the
        derelict L Barn,
    tetrous, pediculous, skint,
    swilling rough cider and Blue.
Now lie we sullenly here in the black mire -
*   this hymn they gurgle,*
* being unable to speak.*
* Here they blaspheme Divine Power.*
Money no object to buyer of L-shaped
**   picturesque old barn**
**   seeking the quiet country life**
    (two hundred and twenty-two grand,
    Property Pages last night -
    with which Mucky Preece is involved,
    scraping the squit from his arse).

terribly sick with her meths, but
she kept on and on vomiting through
the night, but with nothing left to
sick up (the front of her scraggy
overcoat covered in the methsy,
vegetable - soupy slime — the
stench abominable) so that
between honks she screamed hor-
ribly. The only sleep we got was
after one of the old hands dragged
her off, still screaming, and dumped
her in the alley round the corner
where the dustbins are.

Today is <u>Monday</u>: in St. Batolph's
crypt they give out free clothes to us

missiz an me inda warm inda Euston
        unnerground buskin
fugginwell busted armonica playin
        only da one fing
    over an zover again

missiz gone arse-over-ed on da fuggin
        down eshcalator
tryin to swing for some cuntinna bowler
        wot givver two pee
    bazshd up er face an er arm
    cetched up er sleeve in da fing
    where it gozsh clackety-clack
    mergency stop button presh

mashessa blood inna cetchup da coppers
        draggin er screamin
still wiv er good arm out of er pocket
        bockle uv Strongbow

gizzera fifty or twenny fer fuggsay
        mister a tellya
    savvy dis noosepaper see?
    sonly bed we gotter nigh

Remedy

Now that the hanging of murderers has been rejected by Parliament (myself I look upon hanging as barbaric) there is a simple alternative which will give the

They give them too much money to hang about the streets and not to look for work.

They should stop the dole money or cut it in half.

It would stop them

That remedy is to chop off his right leg and his left arm. After all, to give a prisoner a life sentence, he could be out in about 16 years.

EX-SOLDIER
(Name and address supplied)

EX-SOLDIER
(Name and address supplied)

— chop both his arms off. He couldn't do much with his feet.

We come to the person who goes to the dole office and states, by putting his signature to a piece of paper, that he is not working, that done, he then jumps into his car to do a 60 hour week.

The hand that puts his signature to paper should also be chopped off.

Some say they will fight on the beaches. It is a pity they weren't fighting during the war, a bit of army service would do them good.

Cut dole

cut

Gente perduta, wino-unworthies,
        knackered-up dipsos,
    swilling *rosato*-and-meths –
    we snooped a look in their lairs

while they were beachcombing: still-viscid meths-puke,
        faeces, a mattress,
    cardboard, an old plywood door,
    wedged in the clefts of the dunes.

Sweet from the pines wafts a resinous fragrance
        pungent with sea smells
    (molluscs, salinity, kelp);
    regular clank of a bell

tolls from a wreck-buoy, swung by the reflux;
        wardens in green jeeps,
    dapperly-uniformed, plump
    skedaddlers of squatters and tramps,

patrol what aspires to **Reserve of Endangered
        Natural Habitats**;
    a yellow and black JCB
    scrunches shacks into a skip.

author's last review which speaks of 'post-Chernobyl reindeer piled in a ruck in the tundra... trains with their burden of sinister finned flasks [rumbling] ominously on and on through a benighted city where trash amasses, the loonies and dispos [*sic* (presumably dispossessed)] proliferate and the resident strumpet of the Globe opines "If you ask me, this planet is fucked; not just me, love, the whole planet, fucked".' This, scribbled as circumstances permitted, between the derry (derelict house) and St Botolph's crypt where the destitute alcos today. I got some trousers but they had very bad stains down the front and the knees were both in tatters and they stank. The woman in front of me got a yellow vest but said she could see lice and fleas in it and called the vicar a fucking cunt.

Tuesday: In the crypt of St. Botolph's we got a mug of tea and some bits of bread. It's like a sort of air-raid shelter with us all waiting for something awful to go away, or, worse, to happen.

Friday 19th: got some Strongbow with this old shitty dosser, blake

Snarl of a JCB, cordon of Old Bill,
    megaphone rasping
  into a 3 a.m. squat.

Sleep-fuddled dissolutes, still dressing cold dis-
    consolate bratlings,
  struggle with carrier-bags.

One of the Council Bailiffs is sporting a
    Have a Nice Day badge
  fixed on the yellow hard hat.

Often at dusk in the birch woods beyond the
          gates of the city,
you see the glimmer of fires of the hapless
          dispossessed losers.

One of these, russetly lit from beneath by
          fulminant embers,
     howls through the tenebrous gloom -
     something concerning smoked fish,
     black bread and vodka, I think.

Distant, a plangently-played balalaika ac-
          companies wailing
     vocals whose burden is loss -
Gone are the youthfully beautiful whom I
          loved in my nonage;
     strength and vitality, gone;
     roof-tree and cooking-hearth, gone.

Eyes like an elephant's, blood-bleared and tiny,
          gowkily ogle;
tremulous wart-knuckled pachyderm fingers
          fumble a tin cup;
skewers of carp flesh fumed to mahogany;
          dark-crusted rye loaf;
     sloshed spirit hissing in ash.

who, like me, is no stranger to the
pig-pen o' nights, told me how he went
to the Spike last night, but was so
rough still from the surgical spirit
that he fell down the stone stairs and
smashed his face up badly. They told him
to fuck off and come back when he
was better. He did a Skipper last
night on the kitchen window-ledge
of the Royal Hotel — you get a bit of
warmth through the glass — but
the police came round and moved
him on. Tues 23ʳᵈ : The same bloke I was
on about yesterday got given a quid,
so we got this tin of Carlsberg Sp⁻

Don't think it couldn't be you –
   bankrupted, batty, bereft,
huddle of papers and rags in a cardboard
         spin-drier carton,
bottle-bank cocktails and Snow soporifics,
         meths analgesics,
beg-bucket rattler, no-hope no-homer,
         squatter in rat-pits,
   busker in underground bogs
   (plangent the harp-twang, the *Hwaet!*
Haggard, the youthful and handsome whom I
         loved in my nonage;
   vanished, the vigour I valued;
   roof-tree and cooking-hearth, sacked).
   Bankrupted, batty, bereft –
   don't think it couldn't be you.

gizzera quiddora fiftyfer fuggsay
          mistera tellya
tellya da missiziz fugginwell whatnot
          fugginwell ampute
     afer da nackerup arm

armazzerfuggerup der inda Euston
          afera go down
     arse-over-ed in da fing
     waz ish osh clackeshy-clig

missiziz gointer ospical ad da
          whassizname tashun

     tashun da arm as iz skwozsh
     cuts ov da armaziz skwozsh
     nowizza bagwiv one arm
     ospical calls amputaysh

and have been not infrequently
covered in the crusted slurry of the base
beasts with whom I had shared a night's
accommodation.

At about this time yesterday, the St.
Mungo's crowd came round on the soup
run. Nuns called the Poor Sisters of the
Mother of God, or some such crap, dish-
ing us all out with plastic cups of
thin brown broth and a couple of slices
of dry white Mother's Pride. One of the
blokes under the fly-over climbed into
the van and got his dick out. He's
a Brasso addict and was sick
all over the chief nun an

That one is Boris the Swine
(known as 'the Swine' for the fact that he sometimes
        falls in the swine-pen
    when he is terribly drunk –
    covered in slurry for days),
but we must make allowances, since he
        worked at the Station
    when the — remember the headline
(**Efforts are now being made to encase the
        damaged reactor**)?

Often at evening he plangently strums and
        bays from the birch wood,
    where he reposes, this strain:
    Nothing can ever be done;
    things are intractably thus;
all know the bite of grief, all will be brought to
        destiny's issue;
those who have precognition suffer
        sorrow beforehand;
bodies are bankrupt, the main Expedition has
        left us behind it.

┌──────────────────────┐   ┌────────────────────────────
│ **Acute Exposure**   │   │ ꓚᴚꓵꓓƎꓛOᴚꓒ ИOITⱯ
│ **(Gamma Rads)**   │   │ ꓵƎꓒꓕOᴚꓒ ИOITⱯIꓷⱯᴚ
└──────────────────────┘   │ ʇıun   wǝʇsʎs

Widespread experimental work with m
has confirmed the volatile nature of fission p
fault conditions. This was discussed more ful
concluded that for the purpose of overall asse
assume that the gaseous and volatile fission p
tions relative to one and other in which they
xenon, iodine, tellurium, caesium and rutheniu
fission products of importance. From the expe
not appear to be volatile in the conditions of
reasonable accord with the evidence and a reas
to take the release of strontium isotopes, exp
activities of the isotopes present in fuel, as
assumed for the release of gaseous and volatil
activities of important fission products prese
fuel are given in Table II of Lecture No. 6.

DISPERSION OF RADIOACTIVITY IN THE ATMOSPHERE

3.   Pasquill's method of calculating the
in the atmosphere is in use in the U.K.[1].   I
known theoretical treatment by Sutton[2] to gr
empirical correlation of measurements made to
..

Mortality of employees
Energy Authority,

ɼ

    January, 2 a.m.:
at roost on the window-ledge outside a hotel's
        kitchen a dirty
    hirsute in three overcoats
snuggles against frosted glass where a cabbage-
        smelling Vent-Axia
    sussurates vestigial warmth.

Muezzins were Tannoying dirgefully from the
        mosques in the fountained
squares of the Turkish end of the city;
        barbecued goats' smoke
    swealed from ramshackle cafés.

Stallholders (leather and pewterware) tweaked the
        sleeves of the wealthy
Euro/American/Japanese gawpers
        thronging the cramped wynds;
    fezzed coffee-drinkers played chess.

Squatting in alley-muck, whining, a woman
        cradled a frail child;
two other infants with counterfeit blindness,
        rattling beg-bowls,
    obediently foamed at the mouth –

manifest mendicant mountebanks (though their
        glee was authentic
    when you disburdened yourself
    of that frayed ten-dinar note).

Worse than the Shakes is the Horrors — the rats and
　　　echoing voices…

　　　echoing voices
under the flyover, rubble and streets of
　　　boarded-up derries -
No Go for ambulance, fire-brigade, milkman,
　　　Post Office, Old Bill…

　　　when they demolished his sty
　　　Mucky Preece, alias Tucker,
　　　tramped from the sticks to the Borough -
　　　his mother was only a gippo,
　　　his only possession a bucket…

sometimes it seems like a terrible dream, in
　　　which we are crouching
　　　gagged, disregarded, unsought
　　　in dosshouses, derries and spikes,
　　　and from which we shall awake,

　　　mostly it seems, though, we won't.

Unit 4 of the Cher-
c Soviet Union is the
has ever occurred at a
lant, in several respects: in the
f human casualties, in the
released, in the
-strained
' too

14 speech on the
tion confirmed th
week earlier by a
the International /
that the initiating
excursion within t
At the time of th
was at a power le
or 200 MWt. Since
the first two victin
adjustor of a
erator of
ns i

Some workers must have got their skin
contaminated while removing their out
the vault. Improper handling of commu
contamination. From there, the contam
areas around Unit 1 including the Retu
other workers.

Radioactive contamination in the air (

a. Particulate (or dust)

b. Vapour - Iodine, $1H^3$

c. Gaseous - Argon-41, Xe-135, Kr-88

Particulate activity is measured by co
a high efficiency filter and counting
Continuous monitors are of two types.

could have expected that the author himself would have plumbed such depths of filth, depravity and degradation. For, indeed by his own account (the MS Diaries, pp.101–113), he was by this time: 'no stranger to the pig-pen o'nights'; 'not infrequently covered in the crusted slurry of the base beasts with whom [*sic*] [he] had shared a night's accommodation'; 'acquainted with the subtleties of the Bottle–Bank Cocktail, the urinous scent of the squat, the needle's brief oblivion, grief's bite'.

And then, to the indescribable squalor of

Under the concreted cantilevered
         haven of arty
      spans of the *Bibliothek*,
shivering dossers each evening repose in
         newspaper bivvies.
      Mornings, they head for the park.

Slats of the frost-crusted park benches steam in
         8 a.m. sunlight.
      Scavenging corvine-clawed men
rifle each *Abfalleimer*, greedily
         glean after rye crusts
      flung for gross ducks near the lake,

swig the sour dregs of the bottle-bank empties,
         Tafelwein, Schaumwein,
      Spätlese, Steinhäger, Schnapps.
Today I have planted a two-kilo *Schinken*
         where they will find it
      [hooray for the secular saint].

Outside Victoria Station a quorum of
        no-hoper foetid
impromptu imbibers is causing a shindy:
        one of the number,
clutching a bottle of Thunderbird, half-full,
        rolls amongst litter
(chip-papers, Pepsi cans, Embassy packets -
        Indian take-out
    remnants adhere to her mac);
    under one arm is a crutch
    (the other is lopped at the elbow);
plaster encases her leg, which a colleague
        (sipping a Carlsberg)
kicks periodically, bellowing 'fugg-bag,
        fuggbagging fugg-bag'.

1. Radiation Protection

7. Contamination Control

1. Personnel Movement Control

INTRODUCTION

Radioactive contamination may spread f
another in various ways. One of the princi
moving into a contaminated area and trackin
naterial on their clothing, shoes and perso
Various movement control techniques have ev

RADIATION EMERGENCY PROCEDURES | title

Hazard Identification

radiation hazards present in the shutdow
those normally present and those having p
ng retubing activities, are:

Ambient Gamma-fields

nt Gamma-fields are found within the reac
l shutdown conditions. These fields resu
ated components and fuel within the react
mination residing on the interior of pip

Radiation Beams Originating from the

gical shielding normally provides effec
iated with the activated in-core compo
as intense as 300 R/H, may emanate fr
al of a shield plug (S/P) from or of a

Radiation Fields Originating fror
Components and Fuel Removed from

Course ee woz always the Black Sheik of the
        family, ee woz,
    went to une versity too
    (done moths an physicals there),

ad a good job ee did too with that Anat-
        omical Engy,
    then ee dripped out on the dole,
    got on the booze an them dregs

(cococo whatsisname, you know, the white stuff),
        now ees a squitter,
    lives in a squit with no rent,
    eed ad a radio dose.

How doeth the citie sit solitarie that
        was full of people?
She that was great among nations hath no
        comforter, all her
    friends haue dealt treacherously.

Something is in the air, more and more nutters,
        alcos and dossers,
        dole diuturnal.

Sometimes it seems like a terrible dream from
        which we'll awaken;
    but mostly it seems that we won't.

Let us descend, though, through urinous subways to
        miseries greater,
al doloroso ospizio, where the
        newly tormented
        sample new torments.

    Woe vnto them that decree
    vnrighteous decrees and that turn
    the needy from iustice and robbe
    the rights from the poore of my people.

    What will ye doe with yr wealth
    in the day of the storme which shall come
    from afarre, when all that remaines
    is to crouch with those ye haue oppressed?

te Whole Body Doses

Probable Effects

detectable clinical effects.
obably no delayed effects.

ight blood changes with later
covery. Possible nausea.
layed effects possible but
cious effects improbable.

usea and fatigue, possible
omiting. Reduction in certain
lood cells with delayed recov-
ry.

Nausea and vomiting on first
ay. Two week latent period
ollowed by general malaise,
loss of appetite, diarrhea,
moderate emaciation. Possible
death in 2-6 weeks but for
most healthy individuals, re-
covery likely.

Nausea, vomiting, diarrhea in
first hours. Short latent
period followed by epilation,
loss of appetite, general
malaise, then hemmorrhage,
emaciation, purpura, diarrh--
-lammatio of throat
first

Most of them quietly left when the Council
          put in the Bailiffs
     (3 in the morning it was);
     but one nutter stayed there holed up,

stuck his head out of the fourth-storey smashed-paned
          window and hollered
     Don't think it couldn't be you.
     Then he began chucking rats –

ten or a dozen big dead ones (the squat was
          full of them, we found,
     when we moved in with the dozers).
     Queerest thing of the lot

was he came to the window and empted a briefcase
          full of these *papers*,
     hundreds of fluttering sheets
     caught in the wind off the sea,

shipment of radioactive materials,
          health implications,
     Smear Meter, that sort of stuff
     printed on pages ripped out,

radiological half life, atmos-
          pheric dispersal,
     Gamma-fields, Carbon-14,
     blown through the dead silent Borough.

These who have never lived, blind lives so mean they
        envy all others,
    caitiffs whose deep-wailing plaints,
    horrible outcries, hoarse sighs,
Even in duff weather I'd rather do a
        skipper than stop there –
    trouble of kiphouses is
    vermin and no privacy.
piercing the starless air, dark-stained, dolent;
        when I remember,
    terror still bathes me in sweat -
    their thunderous outbreathing of woe.
Hundreds of beds and the blankets is never
        changed off the last one –
    crabs, you can pick up like that.
    No fucking plugs in the sinks.
From the tormented Sad, sigh-troubled breath a-
        rises around them,
    crowds that are many and great,
    children and women and men.
Bloke in the next bed to me (I could see him)
        pissed in his pillow
    then he just slep on it wet.
    Some on em masturbates, loud.
Let us not speak of them, merely observe and
        silently pass by.

Isotope	I-131	Cs-137	Sr-90	Ru-106
				910 rad lung dose to a 6 month old child

inversion neu....
the present Lecture, the cloud-dosag
5×10^{-5} curie-sec/metre^3. Therefore
dosage of gamma activity would be

$$2\cdot011 \times 10^6 \times 5 \times 10^-$$

The dose from a semi-infinite cloud w
according to formula (2). From figur
size of the cloud is $0\cdot38$. Hence the
cloud would be

$$25 \times 0\cdot$$

Again, from Table II of Lecture No. 6
be $0\cdot521 \times 10^6$ curie-MeV. Therefore
filters which retained all the iodine
gamma radiation dose would be reduced

EXTERNAL RADIATION FROM ACTIVITY DEPO

a radiological half life of 5700 years.
a long, long time. Carbon-14 emits a b
of 156 keV. It emits no gamma ray. Th

After the meths she was honking and honking –
        front of the frayed mac
    stippled with vegetal bits,
    Surgical Spirit-beslimed.

In between honks she was screaming and screaming –
        someone has dragged her
    out of the derry back door,
    dumped her where we piss and shit.
    Now we can all get some kip.

or at least seems very likely, that he was given, we do not know by whom, a parcel of 'inside' papers relating to safety procedures during reactor damage and the 'black dust' scare. Since the authorities regarded all matters concerning environmental contamination as Official Secrets, the author's possession and publication (albeit in a form artistically metamorphosed) of certain of these documents was something of a risk. He steadfastly maintained to the police that he had found the material in a trash bucket on the Victoria Line station where he was busking.

That he was now physically and financially derelict ('No stranger to the unstemmable welter of shit') seems to have concentrated his notion of the 'slurry-wallowing degraded dispossessed' as a metaphor for all of *H. sapiens* involuntarily subjected to that other 'excreta' and thereby, irrespective of position in society, dispossessed of

Newspaper, wrapped round the torso between the
    fourth and fifth jerseys
(night attire proper for doing a skipper in
    icy December
    under the Festival Hall),
carries a note to the Editor, from 'Ex-
    Soldier' of Telford,
    outlining plans to withdraw
    DHSS cash from those
    no-fixed-abode parasites.

Wound round a varicose indigo swollen
    leg, between second
    and third pair of trousers (which stink -
    urine and faeces and sick),
Property Pages delineate *bijou*
    River-View Flatlets
    £600,000 each.

How much promethium remains?
Has there been tritium used?

Why did the PM deny there was any
        contamination?
How do they mean to assure
home-owners no risk remains?

What was the level of contamination?
        Where had it come from?
What is a 'Low Level' leak?
Why was the public not told?

Why has the PM consistently issued
        flagrant denials
that any toxin remains
after these secret 'events'?

These are the questions which residents meant to
        raise at the Meeting,
had it materialized.

of the Bottle - Bank cocktail. As
we guzzled this mixture of stuff from
the empties (shaken up in a wine bottle
— a bit sour but OK, only it made us
sick afterwards) he said he used to
work at some atomic power station
(quite posh, he was) but he got the
sack for telling the newspapers about
some radio-active leak, and he'd
stolen all these papers —Top-Secret
— from the Power Station, and he
couldn't get work and then his
wife died (cancer) so he came to
this. I think he was fucking
well crackers, but we all

Week of continuous Blue,
total amnesia, no recollection of
        date or condition,
    skipper or kiphouse or spike,
    contusion and blood on the scalp,
    spew, epilation, the squits,
sight as through flawed glass, misted, contorted,
        nuns from St Mungo's
    doling out dry bread and soup,
    Mucky Preece skinning a cat
    (bashed-in its head with a brick)
    to add to the vegetal stew
    bubbling up in the bucket,
swayingly unzips and waggles his penis,
    ·   smirched with the cat's gore,
urinates into the face of a Blessed
        Sister of Mercy.

[And don't think it couldn't be *you*:
grievously wounded veteran of the
        Battle of Bottle,
    jobless, bereft of home, skint,
down in the cold uriniferous subway
        spattered with drooled spawl,
lying in layers of newspaper ironies –
        Property Prices,
smug To the Editor platitudes on The
        Vagrancy Issue,
    ads for Gonzalez Byass;
dosser with Top Man carrier-bag, en-
        swathed in an *FT*;
Gizzera quiddora fiftyfer fuggsay,
        bankrupted, I been,
    fugginwell bankrupted, me;
    dolent, the wail from the Tube;
    and don't think it couldn't be *you*.]

and 'morose old hypochondriac', as one reviewer dubbed his literary persona — which projected affectation was to become increasingly the reality.

During those last months of inebriate degeneracy (spent under the concrete span of a flyover, in an abandoned skip and in a defunct fibreglass storage bunker — sometime repository of the Borough's rock-salt for icy winter streets), the burden of his monody, rarely coherent, seems to have been Black Dust, 'Pancake' Contamination Meters, Smear Meters, Clean Zones and stochastic risk and *most startling penthouse £2,500,000*

RIVER VIEWS FROM £123,500

VELVET CURTAINS

Sheds

KENNELS

MAINTENANCE FREE STORAGE CONTAINERS

Back of the Maximart, Saturday evenings:
        sometimes they chuck out
edibles (Sell By or Best Before dates of
        which have expired –
     Cheese n' Ham Tasties, Swiss Rolls,
     Ready-to-Microwave-Burgers)
into a skip in the alley.
     Tonight it is minty ice-cream.

Icy December: three rank expendables
        squat on a split tomb
   covered in carroty spew,
one has his cock loose and pisses all over him-
        self and his colleagues –
   steam from both this and their breaths.
Each grasps a 2-litre polythene tub from
        which is extracted
scoopings of green ice by black half-mooned fingers.
        Slurping and beard-smirch,
    guzzle and emerald puke,
punctuate pulls from the communal Blue of
       methyl amnesia.

Wind that disperses the Cloud is a blow for
          Federalism,
fairly enfolding Muskovite, minaret,
          Einkaufszentrum.

Scoffing our tea, bread-and-marge and secreted
          surgical spirit
here in the crypt of St Botolph's it feels like a
          fallout-shelter.

Functional Disturbance of the Gut Fo

After irradiation of the gut in
following disturbances of general fu:
one to two hours:

(1) Nausea and vomiting

This might be thought of as a "r
which stomach contents are dispo
handled by the normal digestive
bably originates in the brain.

(2) Diarrhoea

This is also a rejection phenome
mechanisms.

it was discovered that some of the staff
ject had radioactive contamination on their
estigation it became evident that this form
tected by our "Pancake" contamination meters,
"smear" meters, but not by our older field
foot monitors, nor by the portal monitors.

Please find attached a status report
place ·
number of workers on the Large Scale
had contamination on their skin and c
the hand and foot monitors

Carbon-14 Contamination Problem

Melted-down boot polish, eau de Cologne, meths,
     surgical spirit,
   kerosine, car diesel, derv...

When the St Mungo lot roll up with hot soup,
     what you should do is
   keep back the slice of dry bread;

after they've fucked off, plaster the one side
     thick with the Brasso -
   goes down a regular treat.

   After a gobble of meths,
   crunch up a Trebor Mint fast -
   takes off the heat and the taste.

Piled in a ruck in the tundra a tump of
      Geigering reindeer...

Meanwhile the trains with their sinister finned flasks
      carrying spent rods
  hurtle perpetually on
through the benighted cities where trash a-
      masses and loonies,
alcos and other misfortunates make dole,
      one of whom ventures:
  I think this planet is fucked;
  not just me but the whole planet, fucked.

that she was into the _lot_ - she
kept on about H and Coke and D.D.A.s
and skin-popping and main-lining
and then, when we started to have this
stew I'd made out of the rotten vegetables
they throw away off the stalls in the
market, she threw up straight in
the fire — we'd got a fire going in
the lerry, made out of all the
banisters in the house. Then
someone shouted that the Bailiffs
were coming with the dozers,
and we got all the rats that we'd
killed, and got ready to chuck
them at those bastards with the

Legions of comatose owners of nothing
          under the concrete
      arches are juddered awake,
      impotent, dolent, bereft –

      radioactive spent rods,
bound for reprocessing from the reactors,
          carried in finned flasks,
rumble by railway by night through a city
          hugely unconscious.

      Nothing can ever be done;
      things are intractably thus;
knowing the bite of grief, all will be brought to
          destiny's issue;
those having precognition suffer
          sorrow beforehand.

Grief-bitten impotent owners of nothing,
          holding opinions
      gagged, disregarded, unsought.

Something is in the wind: terrible storms, an
        absence of ozone,
    huge decommission of plants,
    delapse and delapse and delapse...

    10,000 undesired drums
    (3,800 tonnes)
abandoned four-high in a rickety stack that
        pops with expansion,
    sizzles and bubbles and fumes
    fizzing from leaks in the rust
    in the full glare of the sun
200 yards from a shanty camp's tetrous ex-
        pendable tosspots,
    scumbags and alcos and bums.

how the author was last encountered in the
concourse of Euston, pediculous, intoxicated
beyond capability, plunging and bucking like
a demented warhorse — the side of the head
oftentimes cracking against the tiled floor,
blood and contusion already in evidence, a
(profoundly embarrassed and irritated)
companion struggling to hold

Council blokes pulled down the derry and then set
        fire to the floorboards,
rafters and anything else that would burn (the
        squatters of course had
    already burnt all the doors,
    banisters, skirtingboards, stairs).

Those who had formerly dossed there returned that
        night to the bonfire,
Mucky Preece found an old bucket and stewed up
        veg which the market
stallholders chuck in the gutters because it's
        rotten or damaged –
    onions, a turnip, some sprouts.
    The embers were glowing for days.

That's where they found it, singed to the waist, its
        charcoaly leg-sticks
(one of which must have been smashed and remained en-
        cased in cast plaster)
    stuck in still-fulminant ash,
    bits of veg puked on the mac,
    blue meths clutched tight in one claw,
    other limb lopped at the elbow.

Wind that disperses the Cloud (a blow for De-
        mocracy) favours
Palace twerp, propertied yuppie and news-wrapped
        dosser with doses
equal in Geiger croaks. Shreds of (marked **Secret**)
        papers are scuttering
  over the wrecked party-lawn's
  panic-vacated marquee
  and under the Festival Hall,
  drift against cheap sleeping-bags,
  cardboard, plonk bottles and stiffs:

                    rads,

                    stront,

                    risk,

                    leak,

                    contam

Health Implications

Based on the risk estimates
can be concluded that the ri
cancer after irradiation to
from negative to an upper bc
year per rem (Section 2.1).
mulation of extremity dose t
lifetime, it can be shown th
skin cancer is 2.4×10^{-5} pe
risk, based on the 5% case-f
1.2×10^{-6} per rem which is
of the total stochastic risk
Therefore, our calculation i
ICRP's skin weighting factor

inr. ... .c. Some
deaths in . .. weeks, possible
eventual death of 50% of individuals for about 450 rads.

Nausea, vomiting, diarrhea in
first hours. Short latent
period followed by diarrhea,
hemorrhage, purpura, inflam-
mation of throat, fever by
end of first week. Rapid emaciation, and death as early as
2nd week with possible eventual
death of 100% of exposed individuals.

approved by

Carrying on as though nothing is wrong is
        what we are good at:
    incontrovertible end;
    shrieks, lamentations and dole;
    lost livers, roof–trees and hearths;
on the waste ground at the back of the factory
        there's a crone scumbag
    that kips in a big cardboard box,
    etiolated and crushed;
those having precognition suffer
        madness beforehand
(**Efforts are now being made to encase in
        concrete the…**); meanwhile,
here is a factory daily producing
        thousands of badges
        emblazoned with **Have a Nice Day**.

Dusty, crepuscular, vast;
ranks of unfortunate supines fading
        into infinity;
    chamber or bunker or vault
seemingly lacking extremities; coughing,
        puking, diarrhoea;
drone of the crazy invisible exe-
        getist intoning
    Woe vnto woe vnto woe
    vnto woe vnto woe vnto woe

squit
rads

honk
stront

piss
risk

moths
leak

dis   tress
con   tam